DATE DUE

by the same author

plays

PARTY TIME

a screenplay

HAROLD PINTER

faber and faber
LONDON · BOSTON

First published in 1991 by
Faber and Faber Limited
3 Queen Square London WC1N 3AU

Photoset by Parker Typesetting Service, Leicester
Printed in England by Clays Ltd, St Ives plc

A CIP record for this book
is available from the British Library

ISBN 0-571-17005-6

2 4 6 8 10 9 7 5 3 1

To Antonia

Party Time was first performed by the
Almeida Theatre Company on 31 October
1991 at the Almeida Theatre, London.
The cast was as follows:

TERRY	Peter Howitt
GAVIN	Barry Foster
DUSTY	Delia Roche
MELISSA	Dorothy Tutin
LIZ	Tacye Nichols
CHARLOTTE	Nicola Pagett
FRED	Roger Lloyd Pack
DOUGLAS	Gawn Grainger
JIMMY	Harry Burton
Director	Harold Pinter
Designer	Mark Thompson

Party Time was adapted by the author for television in 1992 and was transmitted on 17 November of that year. This is the version published here.

The play was performed by its original cast with the following additions:

SAM	Roland Oliver
PAMELA	Jill Johnson
EMILY	Julie-Christian Young
SUKI	Bridget Lynch Blosse
HARLOW	Kevin Dignam
SMITH	Ben Gray
WAITRESSES	Amelia Blacker and Rebecca Steele

The television production was produced by Michael Custance, designed by Grant Hicks and directed by Harold Pinter.

CHARACTERS

TERRY, a man of forty
GAVIN, a man in his fifties
DUSTY, a woman in her twenties
MELISSA, a woman of seventy
LIZ, a woman in her thirties
CHARLOTTE, a woman in her thirties
FRED, a man in his forties
DOUGLAS, a man of fifty
JIMMY, a young man

SAM, a man in his forties
PAMELA, a woman in her fifties
EMILY, a woman in her thirties
SUKI, a woman in her twenties
HARLOW, a man in his thirties
SMITH, a man in his twenties

1

Gavin's flat.

Sound of a distant helicopter.

People sitting, standing. WAITRESSES *with drinks trays. A bar.*

A large front door.

GAVIN *and* TERRY *standing with drinks.* HARLOW *and* SMITH *listening.*

> TERRY

I tell you, it's got everything.

> GAVIN

Has it?

> TERRY

Oh, yes. Real class.

> GAVIN

Really?

> TERRY

Real class. I mean, what I mean to say, you play a game of tennis, you have a beautiful swim, they've got a bar right there –

GAVIN

Where?

TERRY

By the pool. You can have a fruit juice on the spot, no extra charge, then they give you this fantastic hot towel –

GAVIN

Hot?

TERRY

Wonderful. And I mean hot. I'm not joking.

GAVIN

Like the barber.

TERRY

Barber?

GAVIN

In the barber shop. When I was a boy.

TERRY

Oh yes?

Pause.

What do you mean?

GAVIN

They used to put a hot towel over your face, you see, over your nose and eyes. I had it done thousands of times. It got rid of all the blackheads, all the blackheads on your face.

TERRY

Blackheads?

GAVIN

It burnt them out. The towels, you see, were as hot as you could stand. That's what the barber used to say: 'Hot enough for you, sir?' It burnt all the blackheads out of your skin.

Pause.

I was born in the West Country, of course. So I could be talking only of West Country barber shops. But on the other hand I'm pretty sure that hot towels for blackheads were used in barber shops throughout the land in those days. Yes, I believe it was common practice in those days.

TERRY

Well, I'm sure it was. I'm sure it was. But no, these towels I'm talking about are big bath towels, towels for the body, I'm just talking about pure comfort, that's why I'm telling you, the place has got real class, it's got everything. Mind you, there's a waiting list as long as – I mean you've got to be proposed and seconded, and then they've got to check you out, they don't let any old spare bugger in there, why should they?

GAVIN

Quite right.

TERRY

But of course it goes without saying that someone like yourself would be warmly welcome – as an honorary member.

GAVIN

How kind.

DUSTY *walks through the door and joins them.*

DUSTY

Did you hear what's happened to Jimmy? What's happened to Jimmy?

TERRY

Nothing's happened.

DUSTY

Nothing?

TERRY

Nobody is discussing this. Nobody's
discussing it, sweetie. Do you follow me?
Nothing's happened to Jimmy. And if you're
not a good girl I'll spank you.

DUSTY

What's going on?

TERRY

Tell him about the new club. I've just been
telling him about the club. She's a member.

GAVIN

What's it like?

DUSTY

Oh, it's beautiful. It's got everything. It's
beautiful. The lighting's wonderful. Isn't it?
Did you tell him about the alcoves?

TERRY

Well, there's a bar, you see, with glass
alcoves, looking out to under the water.

DUSTY

People swim at you, you see, while you're
having a drink.

TERRY

Lovely girls.

DUSTY

And men.

TERRY

Mostly girls.

DUSTY

Did you tell him about the food?

TERRY

The cannelloni is brilliant.

DUSTY

It's first class. The food is really first class.

TERRY

They even do chopped liver.

GAVIN

You couldn't describe that as a local dish.

MELISSA *comes through the door and joins them.*

MELISSA

What on earth's going on out there? It's like the Black Death.

TERRY

What is?

MELISSA

The town's dead. There's nobody on the
streets, there's not a soul in sight, apart from
some . . . soldiers. My driver had to stop at a
. . . you know . . . what do you call it? . . . a
roadblock. We had to say who we were . . . it
really was a trifle . . .

GAVIN

Oh, there's just been a little . . . you know . . .

TERRY

Nothing in it. Can I introduce you? Gavin
White – our host. Dame Melissa.

GAVIN

So glad you could come.

TERRY

What are you drinking?

A WAITRESS *approaches.*

Have a glass of champagne.

He hands MELISSA *a glass.*

DUSTY

I keep hearing all these things. I don't know
what to believe.

TERRY

What did you say?

DUSTY

I said I don't know what to believe.

TERRY

You don't have to believe anything. You just
have to shut up and mind your own business,
how many times do I have to tell you? You
come to a lovely party like this, all you have
to do is shut up and enjoy the hospitality and
mind your own fucking business. How many
more times do I have to tell you? You keep
hearing all these things. You keep hearing all
these things spread by pricks about pricks.
What's it got to do with you?

GAVIN (*To* MELISSA)

Come and say hello . . .

He leads MELISSA *away.* TERRY *stares at*
DUSTY.

2

SAM *and* PAMELA.

SAM

I say you've got to keep a sense of proportion.
You can't allow people to get things out of
proportion.

PAMELA

You mean you have to run a tight ship?

SAM

I think you do. Yes, I think you do. You see,
I've always been an absolutely straightforward man.

PAMELA

I can see that.

SAM

Really?

PAMELA

I can see it in your face. And in your stance.
You're straightforward. Quite right. We can't
afford to beat about the bush. We have to ask
direct questions. What is valuable? What is of
value? That is my question. What are the
values we choose to protect and why?

SAM

Quite.

PAMELA

Quite what?

SAM

No, no – I mean – well, yes . . . exactly . . .

3

LIZ *and* CHARLOTTE.

LIZ

So beautiful. The mouth, really. And of
course the eyes.

CHARLOTTE

Yes.

LIZ

Not to mention his hands. I'll tell you, I
would have killed –

CHARLOTTE

I could see –

LIZ

But that bitch had her legs all over him.

CHARLOTTE

I know.

LIZ

I thought she was going to crush him to death.

CHARLOTTE

Unbelievable.

LIZ

Her skirt was right up to her neck – did you
see?

CHARLOTTE

So barefaced –

LIZ

Next minute she's lugging him up the stairs.

CHARLOTTE

I saw.

LIZ

But as he was going, do you know what he
did?

CHARLOTTE

What?

LIZ

He looked at me.

CHARLOTTE

Did he?

LIZ

I swear it. As he was being lugged out he looked back, he looked back, I swear, at me, like a wounded deer, I shall never, as long as I live, forget it, I shall never forget that look.

CHARLOTTE

How beautiful.

LIZ

I could have cut her throat, that nymphomaniac slut.

CHARLOTTE

Yes, but think what happened. Think of the wonderful side of it. Because for you it was love, it was falling in love. That's what it was, wasn't it? You fell in love.

LIZ

I did. You're right. I fell in love. I am in love. I haven't slept all night. I'm in love.

CHARLOTTE

How many times does that happen? That's the point. How often does it really happen? How often does anyone experience such a thing?

LIZ

Yes, you're right. That's what happened to me. That is what has happened – to me.

CHARLOTTE

That's why you're in such pain.

LIZ

Yes, because that bigtitted tart –

CHARLOTTE

Raped the man you love.

LIZ

Yes she did. That's what she did. She raped my beloved.

4

FRED *and* DOUGLAS.

FRED

We've got to make it work.

DOUGLAS

What?

FRED

The country.

Pause.

DOUGLAS

You've brought the house down with that one, Fred.

FRED

But that's what matters. That's what matters. Doesn't it?

DOUGLAS

Oh, it matters. It matters. I should say it matters. All this fucking-about has to stop.

FRED

You mean it?

DOUGLAS

I mean it all right.

FRED

I admire people like you.

DOUGLAS

So do I.

FRED *clenches his fist.*

FRED

A bit of that.

DOUGLAS *clenches his fist.*

DOUGLAS

A bit of that.

5

EMILY *and* SUKI.

EMILY

We're going to Sorley next weekend for the
Horse Trials. The children love it.

SUKI

Is your husband jumping?

EMILY

Well, it's actually the horse that jumps. My
husband is competing.

SUKI

I've watched him jump. He's awfully good.

EMILY *looks at her.*

Well, you know what I mean —

EMILY

You've watched him? Where?

SUKI

Oh, somewhere up north, I think.

EMILY

I'm sure the boys are going to follow in his footsteps. They worship their father.

SUKI

He's not coming here tonight then?

EMILY

Well, of course he's not. He's busy. (*She points to the window.*) Down there.

SUKI

Oh, of course.

6

FRED *and* DOUGLAS.

FRED

How's it going tonight?

DOUGLAS

Like clockwork. Look. Let me tell you something. We want peace. We want peace and we're going to get it.

FRED

Quite right.

DOUGLAS

We want peace and we're going to get it. But we want that peace to be cast iron. No leaks. No draughts. Cast iron. Tight as a drum. That's the kind of peace we want and that's the kind of peace we're going to get. A cast-iron peace.

He clenches his fist.

Like this.

FRED

You know, I really admire people like you.

DOUGLAS

So do I.

They move away. The camera stays looking at the closed front door.

7

HARLOW, SMITH *and* PAMELA.

HARLOW

Mike Harlow.

SMITH

Simon Smith. Assistants to Mr White.

PAMELA

You're Cynthia Harlow's boy.

HARLOW

I am, yes.

PAMELA

We were at Oxford together. Does she still love dogs?

HARLOW

Dogs are her life.

PAMELA

At Oxford she was fully expected to marry a dog.

She studies HARLOW.

She apparently didn't.

8

MELISSA, DUSTY, TERRY *and* GAVIN.

MELISSA (*To* DUSTY)

How sweet of you to say so.

DUSTY

But you do have a really wonderful figure.
Honestly. Doesn't she?

TERRY

I've known this lady for years. Haven't I?
How many years have I known you? Years.
And she's always looked the same. Haven't
you? She's always looked the same. Hasn't
she?

GAVIN

Has she?

DUSTY

Always. Haven't you?

TERRY

She has. Isn't that right?

MELISSA

Oh, you're joking.

TERRY

Not me. I never joke. Have you ever heard me
crack a joke?

MELISSA

No, if I still look all right, it's probably
because I've just joined this new club – (*To*
GAVIN) Do you know it?

TERRY

We were just telling him. We were just telling
him all about it.

MELISSA

Oh, were you?

GAVIN

Just now, yes. Sounds delightful. You're a
member, are you?

MELISSA

Oh yes. I think it's saved my life. The
swimming. Why don't you join? Do you play
tennis?

GAVIN

I'm a golfer. I play golf.

MELISSA

What else do you do?

GAVIN (*Smiling*)

I don't understand what you mean.

TERRY

What else does he do? He doesn't do anything
else. He plays golf. That's what he does.
That's all he does. He plays golf.

GAVIN

Well . . . I do sail. I do own a boat.

DUSTY

I love boats.

TERRY

What?

DUSTY

I love boats. I love boating.

TERRY

Boating. Did you hear that?

DUSTY

I love cooking on boats.

TERRY

The only thing she doesn't like on boats is
being fucked on boats. That's what she
doesn't like.

MELISSA

That's funny. I thought everyone liked that.

GAVIN *and* TERRY *laugh*.

DUSTY

Does anyone know what's happened to my brother Jimmy?

TERRY

I don't know what it is. Perhaps she's deaf or perhaps my voice isn't strong enough or distinct enough. What do you think, folks? Perhaps there's something faulty with my diction. I'm forced to float all these possibilities because I thought I had said that we don't discuss this question of what has happened to Jimmy, that it's not up for discussion, that it's not on anyone's agenda. I thought I had already made that point quite clearly. But perhaps my voice isn't strong enough or perhaps my articulation isn't good enough or perhaps she's deaf.

DUSTY

It's on my agenda.

TERRY

What did you say?

DUSTY

I said it's on my agenda.

TERRY

No no, you've got it wrong there, old darling.
What you've got wrong there, old darling,
what you've got totally wrong, is that you
don't have any agenda. Got it? You have no
agenda. Absolutely the opposite is the case.
(*To the others*) I'm going to have to give her a
real talking to when I get her home, I can see
that.

GAVIN

So odd, the number of men who can't control
their wives.

TERRY

What?

GAVIN (*To* MELISSA)

It's the root of so many ills, you know.
Uncontrollable wives.

MELISSA

Yes, I know what you mean.

TERRY

What are you saying to me?

GAVIN (*To* MELISSA)

I went for a walk in the woods the other day. I
had no idea how many squirrels were still left
in this country. I find them such vivacious

creatures, quite enchanting.

I used to love them as a girl.

Did you really? What about hawks?

Oh I loved hawks too. And eagles. But
certainly hawks. The kestrel. The way it flew,
and hovered, over my valley. It made me cry. I
still cry.

9

*The front door is ajar. The light through it
gradually intensifies. It burns into the room.*

Silhouetted figures moving in foreground.

10

DOUGLAS, FRED, LIZ *and* CHARLOTTE.

DOUGLAS
Oh, have you met my wife?

FRED (*To* LIZ)

How do you do?

LIZ

This is Charlotte.

FRED

We've met before.

LIZ

You've met before?

CHARLOTTE

Oh yes. We've met. He gave me a leg up in life.

DOUGLAS

Did you really? How exciting.

FRED

It was.

DOUGLAS

Was it exciting for you too? To be given a leg up?

CHARLOTTE

Mmmmnnn. Yes. Oh, yes. I'm still trembling.

DOUGLAS

How exciting.

I think this is such a gorgeous party. Don't
you? I mean I just think it's such a gorgeous
party. Don't you? I think it's such fun. I love
the fact that people are so well dressed.
Casual but good. Do you know what I mean?
Is it silly to say I feel proud? I mean to be part
of the society of beautifully dressed people?
Oh, God I don't know, elegance, style, grace,
taste, don't these words, these concepts, mean
anything any more? I'm not alone, am I, in
thinking them incredibly important? Anyway
I love everything that flows. I can't tell you
how happy I feel.

FRED (*To* CHARLOTTE)
You married someone. I've forgotten who it
was.

Long silence.

CHARLOTTE
He died.

Silence.

DOUGLAS
If you're free this summer do come to our
island. We take an island for the summer. Do
come. There's more or less nobody there. Just
a few local people who do us proud. Terribly

civil. Everything works. I have my own generator. But the storms are wild, aren't they darling? If you like storms. Siroccos. Makes you feel alive. Truly alive. Makes the old pulse go rat-at-at-tat. God it can be wild, can't it darling? Makes the old pulse go rat-at-at-tat. Raises the ante. You know. Gets the blood up. Actually, when I'm out there on the island I feel ten years younger. I could take anyone on. Man, woman or child, what?

He laughs.

I could take a wild animal on. But then when the storm is over and night falls and the moon is out in all its glory and all you're left with is the rhythm of the sea, of the waves, you know what God intended for the human race, you know what paradise is.

11

SAM, HARLOW *and* SMITH.

SAM
What is right is right, that's what I say.

HARLOW
Exactly.

SAM

I mean, if a thing works, if a thing is right, respect that, acknowledge it, respect it and hold to it.

SMITH

Hold on to it.

SAM

Hold *to* it. We're talking about principles. I mean, I met a man at a party the other day – I couldn't believe it – He was talking the most absolute bloody crap – his ideas about the world, that kind of thing – he was a complete and utter and total arsehole – a musician or something –

SMITH

Stoddart?

SAM

That's it. Now, you see, these kind of people, they're an infection.

SMITH

Don't worry about Stoddart. We've seen him off.

HARLOW

We've had him for breakfast.

SMITH *and* HARLOW *laugh*.

12

TERRY *and* DUSTY.

TERRY
Are you mad? Do you know what that man
is?

DUSTY
Yes, I think I know what that man is.

TERRY
You don't know what he is. You have no
idea. You don't know what his position is.
You have simply no idea. You simply have no
idea.

DUSTY
He has lovely manners. He seems to come
from another world. A courteous, caring
world. He'll send me flowers in the morning.

TERRY
No he bloody won't. Oh no he bloody won't.

DUSTY
Poor darling, are you upset? Have I let you

down? I've let you down. And I've always tried to be such a good wife. Such a good wife.

They stare at each other.

Perhaps you'll kill me when we get home? Do you think you will? Do you think you'll put an end to it? Do you think there is an end to it? What do you think? Do you think that if you put an end to me that would be the end of everything for everyone? Will everything and everyone die with me?

TERRY

Yes, you're all going to die together, you and all your lot.

DUSTY

How are you going to do it? Tell me.

TERRY

Easy. We've got dozens of options. We could suffocate every single one of you at a given signal or we could shove a broomstick up each individual arse at another given signal or we could poison all the mother's milk in the world so that every baby would drop dead before it opened its perverted bloody mouth.

DUSTY

But will it be fun for me? Will it be fun?

TERRY

You'll love it. But I'm not going to tell you which method we'll use. I just want you to have a lot of sexual anticipation. I want you to look forward to whatever the means employed with a lot of sexual anticipation.

DUSTY

But you still love me?

TERRY

Of course I love you. You're the mother of my children.

DUSTY

Oh incidentally, what's happened to Jimmy?

13

PAMELA, EMILY *and* SUKI.

PAMELA

Oh, I used to play, yes, as a girl. Loved it. My father was a marvellous player. A great smasher at the net.

SUKI

Do you know Robert Cowley? Emily's
husband? The showjumper?

PAMELA

I don't in fact *know* him, but –

SUKI

He's a wonderful tennis player. (*To* EMILY)
Isn't he?

EMILY

He's top of the ladder at the club.

PAMELA

Ladder?

EMILY

Yes, the tennis ladder at the club – you know
– our club – he's top of the ladder.

SUKI

Swingeing forehand. Literally swingeing.

EMILY

Well, actually he is in fact a totally
accomplished all-round athlete.

SUKI

Doesn't he jump for the army?

EMILY *stares at her*.

PAMELA (*To* EMILY)
You must be so proud.

14

FRED *and* CHARLOTTE.

FRED
Such a long time.

CHARLOTTE
Such a long time.

FRED
Isn't it?

CHARLOTTE
Oh, yes. Ages.

FRED
You're looking as beautiful as ever.

CHARLOTTE
So are you.

FRED
Me? Not me.

CHARLOTTE

Oh, you are. Well, in a manner of speaking.

FRED

What do you mean, in a manner of speaking?

CHARLOTTE

Oh, I meant you look as beautiful as ever.

FRED

But I never was beautiful. In any way.

CHARLOTTE

No, that's true. You weren't. In any way at all. I've been talking shit. In a manner of speaking.

FRED

Your language was always deplorable.

CHARLOTTE

Yes. Appalling.

FRED

Are you enjoying the party?

CHARLOTTE

Best party I've been to in years.

Pause.

FRED

You said your husband died.

CHARLOTTE

My what?

FRED

Your husband.

CHARLOTTE

Oh my husband. Oh yes. That's right. He died.

FRED

Was it a long illness?

CHARLOTTE

Short.

FRED

Ah.

Pause.

Quick then.

CHARLOTTE

Quick, yes. Short and quick.

Pause.

FRED

Better that way.

CHARLOTTE

Really?

FRED

I would have thought.

CHARLOTTE

Ah. I see. Yes.

Pause.

Better for who?

FRED

What?

CHARLOTTE

You said it would be better. Better for who?

FRED

For you.

CHARLOTTE *laughs.*

CHARLOTTE

Yes! I'm glad you didn't say him.

FRED

Well, I could say him. A quick death must be better than a slow one. It stands to reason.

CHARLOTTE

No it doesn't.

Pause.

Anyway, I'll bet it can be quick and slow at the same time. I bet it can. I bet death can be both things at the same time. Oh by the way, he wasn't ill.

Pause.

FRED

You're still very beautiful.

CHARLOTTE

I think there's something going on in the street.

FRED

What?

CHARLOTTE

I think there's something going on in the street.

FRED

Leave the street to us.

CHARLOTTE

Who's us?

FRED

Oh, just us . . . you know.

She stares at him.

CHARLOTTE

God, your looks! No, seriously. You're still so handsome! How do you do it? What's your diet? What's your regime? What *is* your regime by the way? What do you do to keep yourself so . . . I don't know . . . so . . . oh, I don't know . . . so trim, so fit?

FRED

I lead a clean life.

DOUGLAS *and* **LIZ** *join them.*

CHARLOTTE (*To* **DOUGLAS**)

Do you too?

DOUGLAS

Do I what?

CHARLOTTE

Fred says he looks so fit and so . . . handsome
. . . because he leads a clean life. What about
you?

DOUGLAS

I lead an incredibly clean life. It doesn't make
me handsome but it makes me happy.

LIZ

And it makes me happy too. So happy.

DOUGLAS

Even though I'm not handsome?

LIZ

But you are. You are. Isn't he? He is. You are.
Isn't he?

DOUGLAS *puts his arm around her.*

DOUGLAS

When we were first married we lived in a
two-roomed flat. I was – I'll be frank – I was a
traveller, a commercial traveller, a salesman –
it's true, that's what I was and I don't deny it
– and travel I did. Didn't I? Travel I did.
Because my little girl here had given birth to
twins.

He laughs.

Can you believe it? Twins. I had to slave my guts out, I can tell you. But this girl here, this little girl here, do you know what she did? She looked after those twins all by herself! No maid, no help, nothing. She did it herself – all by herself. And when I got back from my travelling I would find the flat immaculate, the twins bathed and in bed, tucked up in bed, fast asleep, my wife looking beautiful and my dinner in the oven.

FRED *applauds.*

And that's why we're still together.

He kisses LIZ *on the cheek.*

That's why we're still together.

15

HARLOW *and* SMITH *walk through the empty hall. The front door is closed. They stop, look down the corridors and then go out of shot. The camera follows them, then slowly pans back to the front door. It is now ajar. The light through it gradually intensifies. It burns into the room.*

16

TERRY, DUSTY, GAVIN, MELISSA, FRED, CHARLOTTE, DOUGLAS, LIZ, SAM, PAMELA, EMILY, SUKI, HARLOW *and* SMITH.

TERRY

The thing is, it is actually real value for money. Now this is a very, very unusual thing. It is an extremely unusual thing these days to find that you are getting real value for money. You take your hand out of your pocket and you put your money down and you know what you're getting. And what you're getting is absolutely gold-plated service. Gold-plated service in all departments. You've got real catering. You've got catering on all levels. You've not only got very good catering in itself – you know, food, that kind of thing – and napkins – you know, all that, wonderful, first rate – but you've also got artistic catering – you actually have an atmosphere – in this club – which is catering artistically for its clientele. I'm referring to the kind of light, the kind of paint, the kind of music, the club offers. I'm talking about a truly warm and harmonious environment. You won't find voices raised in our club. People don't do vulgar and sordid and offensive things. And if they do we kick them in the balls and chuck them down the stairs with no trouble at all.

Can I subscribe to all that has just been said?

Pause.

I would like to subscribe to all that has just been said. I would like to add my voice. I have belonged to many tennis and swimming clubs. Many tennis and swimming clubs. And at some of these clubs I first met some of my dearest friends. All of them are now dead. Every friend I ever had. Or ever met. Is dead. They are all of them dead. Every single one of them. I have absolutely not one left. None are left. Nothing is left. What was it all for? The tennis and the swimming clubs? What was it all for? What?

Silence.

But the clubs died too and rightly so. I mean there is a distinction to be made. My friends went the way of all flesh and I don't regret their passing. They weren't my friends anyway. I couldn't stand half of them. But the clubs! The clubs died, the swimming and the tennis clubs died because they were based on ideas which had no moral foundation, no moral foundation whatsoever. But *our* club, *our* club – is a club which is activated, which is inspired by a moral sense, a moral awareness, a set of moral values which is – I have to say – unshakeable, rigorous, fundamental, constant. Thank you.

Applause.

17

Phone ringing. HARLOW *picks it up.*

HARLOW
Yes? . . . Thank you.

He puts the phone down.

18

The group.

GAVIN
Yes, I'm terribly glad you've said all that.

HARLOW *approaches* GAVIN *and whispers in his ear.* GAVIN *nods and turns to the others.*

Aren't you?

DOUGLAS

First rate.

LIZ

So moving.

PAMELA

Absolutely right!

TERRY

Fantastic.

EMILY

Lovely!

FRED

Right on the nail.

SUKI

Spot on!

CHARLOTTE

So true.

SMITH

Great.

DUSTY

Oh yes.

She claps her hands.

Oh yes.

SAM

Terrific.

DOUGLAS

Absolutely first rate.

GAVIN

Yes, it was first rate. And it desperately
needed saying. And how splendid that it was
said tonight, at such an enjoyable party, in
such congenial company. I must say I speak as
a very happy host. And by the way, I'll really
have to join this wonderful club of yours,
won't I?

TERRY

You're elected forthwith. You're an honorary
member. As of today.

Laughter and applause.

GAVIN

Thank you very much indeed. Now I believe
one or two of our guests encountered traffic
problems on their way here tonight. I
apologize for that, but I would like to assure
you that all such problems and all related
problems will be resolved very soon. Between
ourselves, we've had a bit of a round-up this

evening. This round-up is coming to an end. In fact normal services will be resumed shortly. That is, after all, our aim. Normal service. We, if you like, insist on it. We will insist on it. We do. That's all we ask, that the service this country provides will run on normal, secure and legitimate paths and that the ordinary citizen be allowed to pursue his labours and his leisure in peace. Thank you all so much for coming here tonight. It's been really lovely to see you, quite smashing.

WAITRESSES *enter with champagne.*
Laughter. A tumult of voices.

19

Laughter continuing. Shifting bodies. At the very far end of the hall the front door can be seen. It is wide open. The light burns into the room. A young man stands in the frame of the door. He is thinly dressed.

The camera moves through the crowd towards him. The sounds die.

JIMMY
Sometimes I hear things. Then it's quiet.

I had a name. It was Jimmy. People called me Jimmy. That was my name.

Sometimes I hear things. Then everything is quiet. When everything is quiet I hear my heart. When the terrible noises come I don't hear anything. Don't hear don't breathe am blind.

Then everything is quiet. I hear a heartbeat. It is probably not my heartbeat. It is probably someone else's heartbeat.

What am I?

Sometimes a door bangs, I hear voices, then it stops. Everything stops. It all stops. It all closes. It closes down. It shuts. It all shuts. It shuts down. It shuts. I see nothing at any time any more. I sit sucking the dark.

It's what I have. The dark is in my mouth and I suck it. It's the only thing I have. It's mine. It's my own. I suck it.